Managing Stress In The Workplace

How To Get Rid Of Stress At Work And Live A Longer Life

Joe Martin

2nd Edition with Bonus Chapters

D1059230

First Published, 2014

Dedication

To all the workaholics on the planet

Table of Contents

Conclusion

About the Author

Joe Martin is a life coach.

Earlier, he had set up a few businesses and sold them. He has a knack for writing and hence he became a full time writer. He has started his writing career with a hope to change lives.

When he is not working, he enjoys travelling, fishing, cooking and reading books. He loves to play with his two daughters when he is home.

He was featured on Google News, Yahoo Finance, Business Insider, The Boston Globe, CBC Money Watch and other popular media channels.

Introduction

Workers worldwide are going through a turbulent phase because of the troubled economy. Words like 'redundancy', 'cut-backs' and 'lay-offs' have become very common. This has resulted in increased levels of stress, anxiety, fear and job insecurities. Workplace stress severely increases during times of economic crisis; hence, it is very essential to learn innovative ways of coping with the building pressure. Mastering the ability to manage workplace stress can make a huge difference between job failure and success. The more you manage your stress levels at the workplace, the more positively you will affect the ones around you.

During these times of economic crisis, it may seem very difficult to cope with the challenges and disputes that arise in the workplace. Workers, managers and employers, irrespective of the industry, are all suffering from aggravated levels of stress;

we take stress with us from home and the commute, and more stress awaits us when we get to our jobs. A certain amount of everyday stress is normal; however, excessive distress hampers our productivity, our emotional and physical health, and our working relationships.

Diminishing stress at the workplace is crucial for maintaining your overall health, as it can promote longevity, boost your immune system, and help you in being more productive. Never let your stress get the best of you, because if you do, you not only put yourself at the risk of developing several life-threatening ailments, but you also risk failure.

Stress has a massive impact on your overall wellbeing because it is a natural response activated in the brain. It is therefore essential that you learn ways to keep your stress levels under control at your workplace. Fortunately, there are many effective ways to reduce or eliminate stress at work, and in this book, we will discuss in great detail why stress affects you the way it does, the repercussions of leading a stressful life, and the various ways to combat it successfully.

Chapter 1

A LATENT GLOBAL EPIDEMIC

"WORKPLACE STRESS"

"It is the usual story. Holding down a job, doing up a home, chairing the Board of Governors at the local comprehensive... it was only in the hospital that I realized how exhausted I was..."

These were the words uttered by Valerie Yates, who had decided to quit her job – sorry, her 'stressful job' – as a marketing director and college board member in Chicago, after she was diagnosed with breast-cancer back in 1997. Fortunately, Mrs. Yates is healthy now, and she gladly admits, "Being away from the office helped me see how stressful and unhealthy it was, how unhealthy – and how much I hated my boss." She adds with a smile of relief, "Life was too short to spend it somewhere like that."

That was in 1997. We are in a whole new era now. However, what Mrs. Yates had suffered back then has now become a part and parcel of our everyday lives. Increasing demands for work efficiency, work output and rising workload have for many employees made the terms 'work' and 'stress' synonymous, which is a sad but hard-hitting truth. If you, my friend, think that you are a victim of stress at your workplace, realize that you are not alone.

Stress at work is now a worldwide phenomenon. Up from a 73% of workers in America in 2012, 84% workers in 2013 had admitted to being stressed by their jobs, according to a 2013 study conducted by Harris Interactive for Everest College, which was published in the November 2013 issue of Forbes magazine. Furthermore, 14% of workers pegged 'low salary' as the leading cause of stress, while 'unreasonable workload' stood a close second, followed by 11% of the workers citing 'commuting' and 'annoying co-workers.' Other stress stimulants included: fear of being fired (4%), lack of opportunity for advancement (6%), poor work-life balance (7%), and the job itself not being the primary career choice (8%). The survey had also revealed that those of the millennial generation –i.e., ages 18 to 29 – tended to express more stress, largely caused by job stability concerns.

In June 2013, the American Psychological Association in New York produced a report that presented the results of their research on increasing stress complaints. According to the report, the data stands as:

Impacts of Stress at Workplace	Average of Victims
People who regularly experience physical symptoms caused by stress	77%
Regularly experience psychological symptoms	73%
Feel thay are living with extreme stress	33%
Feel their stress has increased over past 5 years	48%

That's not all. In addition, the survey also brought to light some of the common symptoms of elevated stress at the workplace, such as anxiety and nervousness (cited by 45% of the workers), lack of energy (45%), irritability and anger (50%), and wanting to cry for relief (35%).

A small glimpse of the large side effects of stress

An old axiom goes like this – "a happy worker is a productive worker." Stress takes its toll not only on individuals, but also on the quantitative and qualitative productivity of firms, companies and workplaces, since these very 'individuals' are their building blocks.

Work-related stress caused workers in Great Britain to lose 10.4 million working days in 2012 and 2013, based on the Labor Force Survey (LFS) conducted by the Office for National Statistics (ONS).

In Canada, data shows that stress-related absenteeism has cost employers losses of $15 to $25 billion in 2012-2013, compared to $3.5 billion in 2003. Roughly 500,000 Canadian workers are absent from the workplace each day due to mental and health-related workplace stress issues. Simultaneously, stress also accounts for 60% of workplace accidents, 19% of absenteeism, 30% of short and long-term disability, and a reduction in turnover of up to 40%.

Chapter 2

AN INTRODUCTION- TO YOUR DAILY 'NECESSARY EVIL'

I am sure you would not disagree that stress is an inevitable part of your everyday 'work' life. You simply cannot ignore it.

However, I suggest you to first view stress as a stimulant. See, stress can motivate a person to be productive and to rise up to face the challenge of tough situations.

Needless to say, we live amidst competing times, and to survive the competition, one always needs to be at the edge. Stress as a positive phenomenon does exactly that – it keeps you on the edge.

However, having said that, we must keep in mind that anything too much or exceeding its limits is negative. For lovers of literature, remember Shakespeare's Macbeth? Too much ambition resulted in an untimely doom. Stress can do exactly that, and often much more.

'Workplace stress is defined as a harmful reaction that people have to endure the pressures and demands placed on them at work.'

The main causes of workplace stress are attributed to work pressure, work-related bullying or violence, and often, lack of managerial support.

These factors cause a 'burnout,' leading to a breakdown, either psychological or physical. You may ask what I mean by 'burnout'. That is exactly what you should do first – ask questions— and talk to yourself regarding your workplace stress patterns. We will follow up this entire study with an elaborate synopsis regarding symptoms, remedies and solutions for stress.

Coming back to burnout, in short, 'stress burnout' is a deep-seated sense of disillusionment and exhaustion with a job or career that used to provide much excitement and motivation. Enthusiasm and passion are gradually stripped away until the drive and will to go on are lost.

I can already see many of you connecting to it. By this time, most of you may now understand that 'stress' is a necessary evil. It is an inevitable part and parcel of your daily lives – a necessary kick to keep you on your toes and allow you to excel. But nevertheless, when it deprives you of your 'life,' it turns evil.

Understanding workplace stress and realizing your limits in enduring it are the most essential steps in your fight against it. So now that you all know what 'stress' is, you are one step closer to controlling it, just like how doctors who can diagnose an illness can proceed down a definite path to treating it.

Chapter 3

TRY AND UNDERSTAND THE PROBLEM

Once you have admitted that you are a victim of stress at the workplace, it becomes easy to combat stress because now you are 'aware' of your position.

Grab a pen and a paper. Try to realize what exactly the reason for your stress is. It may be one cause or more.

Write them down on the paper. You can always use a notebook or an iPhone, android or tablet to type and save the problems; but remember, nothing can replace the art of writing.

When you write, your muscles tend to relax. Your mind focuses on the writing. Now this is very important, because when you are calm, you can recollect, reason and recognize the causes of stress properly.

Yes, writing is a healthy way to keep cool. While writing down the causes of your stress, leave some space beside each one. Whenever you find a possible solution, make an entry on the paper.

Keep the papers with you at all times, especially during office hours, and see that you adhere to the solutions you have written.

There are some common causes of stress. Through a few discussions with some of my friends, I have made a rough idea of what most employees go through. Here on, we will see some prevailing causes of stress and try to work our ways through them for an effective solution.

TOO MANY PROBLEMS? SO ARE THE SOLUTIONS

Workplace stress may not only remain within the boundaries of your office, but also tag along into your personal life. This is one of the psychological hazards of workplace stress.

Another hazard is that it is embedded in the office itself, disguised as work demand, output, meeting the target, deadlines, and so on. In addition to all of these, there are physical hazards too. Violence, work abuse, offensive co-workers, or a bully boss can take a toll on your physical health.

The 'A-class' treatment to your stress problems starts right here – Aware, Analyze, Apply. Being aware is realizing that you are stressed by observing the symptoms, such as headaches, nervousness, excessive worry, increased irritability, and fatigue. You may also realize that you are starting to avoid people and social engagements.

The next step is analysing the causes of stress correctly. Once you know the causes, it is time to apply the appropriate solutions. These three steps form the basis of any kind of planning to combat stress.

Do not get disheartened. For each and every one of these, you can follow a simple "4-As" solution.

1. Avoid
2. Alter
3. Adapt
4. Accept

Remember, every problem has its own unique solution, just like every lock has its key. But these 4 A's are the master key to your solutions to stress in your workplace. There is no reason to go head-on in every matter. You will not become a hero but a victim.

Let's start with the first A – Avoid unnecessary situations.

When you cannot avoid, try to Alter. Change your approach; change your attitude towards the problem and the way to deal with it. Alter your approach to different kinds of people. Do not use the same approach for your co-workers that you use for your boss.

The next two – Adapt and Accept – are on the same plane. Sometimes, you need to accept certain situations and adapt accordingly. Learn to forgive and forget, and try to anticipate by choosing your interpretation of a situation in a more appropriate way.

As we discuss, it will become clearer which of the 4-A's is suitable in which situations.

Chapter 4

UNLOAD THE WORKLOAD

A lot of you must have faced, and are surely still facing, the pressure of an increasing workload, are you not?

Files are piling up, incomplete data-sheets are lying around on your desk, the clock is ticking like a time-bomb, and the screen on your laptop is waiting for your next click... what a situation! Can it get any worse than this? Oh yes! Your boss calls and hands over another set of tasks with another deadline.

Relax. The easiest way to set things right is by planning. First of all, what you need to do is TIME MANAGEMENT. Yes, divide your work and set time limits. What aids you in this is planning ahead.

Go to work early and have a glass of water. Relax yourself and see which tasks are pending.

Devote necessary time to each of them as per required, with small five-minute breaks in between. These breaks will help you to relax and revitalize for the next set of tasks.

Utilize your time management skills to shuffle and arrange the data sheets, files and computer programs under common genres. Arrange in separate folders if necessary. Plan and approach, but do not forget to set the proper time limit. This will prevent jumping from one type of work alignment to another.

Believe me, – as one by one, a stack of files or a task is completed, you will breathe a sigh of relief and gain enthusiasm to solve the next one. But do not forget to take small breaks in between.

The next important step is PRIORITIZE. Arrange your tasks according to their importance. Irrespective of whether you like the work for a particular task or not, complete it if it is to be submitted early.

If you are working and you suddenly get a call from your boss asking you to complete a file, do it right then and get it over with. This will keep the boss in good humor and earn you respect.

If you leave the work for later, it will be an added burden and keep distracting you in the back of your mind, and may even interfere with your time management routine. So prioritize your tasks and then take a step forward.

Concentrate on a 'step by step' format

The mind has a limited capacity. If you keep pressuring it and pushing its boundaries, you will surely feel stressed. It is only fair that you concentrate on one goal at a time. Whenever you have a big, elaborate assignment, do not try to complete the whole thing at once. Divide it into parts, and focus on each part with individual details. Follow the 'step by step' format. This will not only allow you to avoid getting stressed, but also make you more productive.

Set a clear objective for yourself

Sometimes, when you do not know where you are going, doubts begin to arise and the tension mounts, leading to a lot of stress. To avoid such pit-falls, it is very important that you set a clear-cut objective before you start working.

Define the objective

This way, you will have an idea of the 'result' you will be working to achieve.

For example, if the assignment involves providing annual data for your workplace, your objective should be to produce a monthly study of the company's profit and loss. Concentrate on each month individually and its turnover. Then provide a chart to compare the monthly and average profits and losses for the whole year. Remember, your mind influences your actions.

So, if you have a planned mindset, your actions will comply with it and give you the desired results.

The next step is something most of us are reluctant to do. Some of you may have guessed it, but it is the time to say 'NO'. See, everyone cannot do everything every time. Do not see this as a drawback. No one is questioning your abilities if you say 'No'. If you already feel burdened with your current work, a heap of additional work will definitely send you off the roof.

Also, accepting a task and not completing it will cause a blot on your performance. This is what you should do – politely give the valid explanation behind your 'No'. Ask your boss to help you out if you do not understand or have any queries regarding the assigned work. Accepting your problem, admitting it and asking for help from your superior will be beneficial to you. Firstly, you will gain respect. Secondly, you can learn from your superior. You may also develop a good work relationship. Judge for yourself, my friend – what will be better for you? Taking an assignment, not completing it and enduring the rage of your boss? Or, saying 'NO' now, then taking on the task when you are capable to handle and complete it, thereby getting goodwill? It is not so tough to choose, is it?

Remember, you can either change the situation or change your course to respond to the situation. 'Focus' is most essential.

1. Focus on what you must do and then what you should do to meet it.
2. Focus on your strengths and how to take care of your drawbacks.

Planning, time management, setting the targets in sequential order according to 'must do' and 'should do', and saying 'no' in the right way will all release you from your stressful position, and that is exactly our goal.

Chapter 5

BE 'AWARE'-

KNOW WHAT YOUR POSITION IS

Stop! Think! Your work is stressing you out, but is it worth it? There are a lot of questions that require your attention, and answering them will help you realize exactly how much pressure you should be feeling in your position at the workplace, and how much extra is burdening you.

Ask yourself, is your commitment towards your work valued? If you are dedicating 8 to 10 hours daily to your work, is your hard work being recognized by higher authorities? If not, ask them for feedback regarding your work, and question them on how you can improve, if it is necessary.

This showcases a positive attitude and seriousness towards your occupation; it will also register you in the 'good' books of your seniors. Secondly, when an assignment or a group task is given to you, clarify the ROLE you are supposed to take on.

Do not, I repeat, do not take on unnecessary burdens by trying to do more than required. Consult your supervisor; ask if you are to be an interpreter, an advisor, or a planner for the assignment. For example, if a group task is given, consider your options. See that you do something substantial. Be the advisor, or be the planner, and work on the layout of the project. If you are comfortable with the layout then make a list, consulting with your group, and gather necessary items and assemble them.

But do not be an architect *and* a planner *and* an interpreter. It will spill the milk.

Thirdly, as I mentioned, see that you are doing something substantial. Ask yourself – is my job or my work meaningful? If yes, then how is it meaningful? If no, then how can I make it better? Often times, we feel depressed when after hours of hard work, we do not get the desired results. Does that mean that you, I, we are all failures? Not at all. What it does mean is that our work may not have been recognized. Approach your supervisor or superior and calmly present your work. Make them take notice of your effort. At least you will be glad that you tried your best. Feeling good about yourself will help reduce the stress.

Next, ask one important question – what are your POSSIBILITIES for DEVELOPMENT? Think of your development as an individual and as an employee, and how your work environment can accelerate your growth. If you find that your work environment is not suitable, consider altering it. How can you better yourself in this environment? Should you change your workplace? Consider your options carefully. Remember, progress can never be stagnant; it is progressive.

The most important question to be considered is regarding DISCRIMINATION. Discrimination based on color, status and sex is equivalent to criminal assault. If you are a victim, do not be scared or depressed. Remember, you can approach the judicial doors; it is your right. Know your company's policies and procedures properly. Keep a hard copy in your bag. Whenever you feel harassment owing to discrimination, contact your superior and highlight the policies on discrimination. If things do not improve, document all conversations with your co-workers and boss, be it verbal or via email or messages.

You can consult your HR or a jury, if needed, with substantial evidence. The Civil Rights Act makes it illegal to discriminate on grounds of class, race, gender, color, religion or national origin. Hence, know your 'position'. As a responsible citizen, you deserve equal treatment, so know your rights. There is nothing shameful about asking for what is rightfully yours.

Chapter 6

COMBAT TO COORDINATION

WITH 'CO' WORKERS

Well, let's admit it, co-workers and colleagues can often be the biggest threat to a peaceful work environment. Since they come with the tag of 'co' (together), handling co-workers and colleagues can turn into a tricky situation.

Nevertheless, bullying, verbal or physical abuse, undesired sexual attention and emotional harassment can often create a disgusting cause for stress at the workplace. Let us find out how we can avoid some of these situations.

First of all, avoid unpleasant situations. What I mean is, do not get yourself involved in unnecessary arguments. Excuse yourself.

For example, if three or four of your co-workers are arguing over a topic and they call upon you to join, politely reply that they have a better understanding of the topic in discussion and that they can contribute more than you do. Or, excuse yourself by saying that you need to make a call or visit the washroom.

Remember, by getting involved in unnecessary discussions and heated arguments, you paint a 'target' on yourself. At times, a situation may arise in which a colleague is constantly on your back. You decide to change the situation, and you have two ways of doing this; first, you can move your desk and sit at a different place, or second, talk to your supervisor for help.

If your senior or your boss is the bully, what do you do? The most essential thing is to not get involved in his bullying antics, such as screaming or arguing or a head-on clash. He actually wants you to react that way. It will dampen your reputation and prestige in the workplace, whereas the boss stands with nothing much to lose. After he has bullied you, just say a 'thank you' and leave. Nothing will be more insulting to him than your silence and negligence. He will find someone else to bully and entertain himself. Remember this, "You don't wrestle with a pig because the pig loves to get muddy".

Resolving conflicts in healthy, constructive ways can strengthen trust and relieve workplace stress. If a co-worker has any issues with you, take the initiative and talk. Don't think, "Why should I approach first?" Instead, think, "How can I resolve this quickly?" Have a talk alone with the co-worker and ask him/her what problem she/he has with you and how you can solve it. If the person is emotionally charged, it's always clever to stay focused on the present and not talk of old resentments and hurts. Go for a new beginning. If a conflict cannot be resolved at the very moment, choose to end the discussion, even if you still disagree. Take it up later at a more favorable time.

You can further implement some small changes that may give happy rewards. Humor is a great stress buster when used appropriately. When the environment gets too stressed, find a way to lighten the mood by sharing a joke, or maybe a funny incident with your co-workers. Develop a friendship with some of your colleagues. Remember to offer them support when they need it. This way, if someone else bullies you, your co-workers will stand by you. Sometimes, go for mutually shared humor to ease tensions. However, be cautious; if the laugh comes at someone else's expense, it may elevate the stress for you.

When you are working on an assignment, discuss a few points with your co-workers. This does not mean you have to implement their ideas and views; it is more of a tactic for good bonding. Your co-workers will feel that you treat them with respect and equality. Lunch hour discussions on various topics like cricket, sports, and movies can create a light and stress-free environment. Also, when you use the coffee machine or make a cup of tea for yourself, make a few extra for your colleagues. It shows warmth, no not of the tea, but yours. You may be delighted to see, a few days later, your colleagues returning the favor.

So take a step forward. A bit of adaption and alteration will go a long way in easing workplace stress in your favor.

Chapter 7

WHEN THE JOB ITSELF
BECOMES THE STRESS

A lot of employees and workers have admitted that the job itself is the biggest cause of stress. For a good 20% of employees, their job is not of their own choosing, but for a livelihood.

Every year, there is a widespread trend of employees switching from one job to another due to the lack of job satisfaction. The following discussion will shed light on some of the cautions that one should keep in mind when you are stressed due to the job itself.

Terms like 'lay-offs' and 'budget cuts' have become common in the workplace environment. So when your salary creates a problem for you, there are 3 different paths to take.

The first, and the easiest, is to remove yourself from the current workplace. The second option is to ask for a raise. Talk it out with your superiors, explain your point and back it up with valid reasons. Or, take the third option – accept your present position and move on. But whatever you do, be clear about it. Carry on your career, not your stress.

The next scenario involves the work-family balance. Many people tend to carry their work home with them, together with the stress and burdens of the workplace; in such cases, their family is the worst sufferer.

Here is what you can do:

Make it a point to hold a lighthearted family meeting on every weekend. Discuss the upcoming events of the week ahead and plan your schedule accordingly so that you do not miss out on any important occasion.

1. Have dinner together with other members of your family, especially your spouse and children.

2. Share your workplace experience with your spouse, and attentively give time to her when she shares the events of her day.

3. Try to walk your children to school or drop them off on your way to work. During this time, have a hearty laugh and show your warmth and love towards them. This will also serve as a happy relief for you when you visualize it during stressful situations.

4. Try your best to attend important family occasions such as your parents' anniversary, your anniversary, your children's birthday, and their special days at school.

5. Most importantly, keep your work outside when you enter your home. No matter how little time you get with your family, convert it into quality time. This

feeling of happiness will prove to be one of the greatest stress busters for you at your workplace.

It always feels good when you have someone to share your burden or at least understand your problems. Talk to somebody who has overcome such stressful situations. However, it is advised not to talk to anyone who is sharing your workplace, as it may send a negative message. You can talk to a counselor and have a few sessions to help you cope with workplace stress. This will help you to shun any rising negative feelings surrounding your workplace.

If nothing else is working and you are adamant on changing your workplace or career itself, a few necessary precautions should be considered.

1. The positive impact of changing your job will be that your skills and previous experiences that you have acquired will be transferrable and will allow you to re-dedicate your original goals by starting anew.

2. Besides job satisfaction, the primary consideration while switching jobs should be that your economic level of subsistence must not decrease abruptly.

3. However, competition may arise from younger employees who might be ready to work for a much lower salary, thus affecting your bargaining power.

4. Ask yourself – is the job itself the reason for my stress? Or is it the boss or my co-workers? If it is the job or the lifestyle related to the job, then merely changing the workplace to another with the same job conditions will give rise to similar stressful conditions.

Chapter 8

YOUR PERSONAL ARMORY TO BATTLE STRESS

Yoga

Scientific studies have established a number of positive effects yoga has on the nervous system, brain and immune system. Yoga also relaxes the mind, as true relaxation is when the body and mind are in a state of balance. Practicing yoga before leaving for work or during lunch hour before having your lunch can prove beneficial in relieving stress. Now, I am not an expert, but here is a quick list of some of the impacts of yoga.

1. Standing postures improve blood and fluid circulation to lower areas of the body, and they also strengthen leg muscles;

2. Inverse positions, like the headstand, increase the flow of blood to the heart, lungs and brain;

3. Forward bends are beneficial for cooling blood pressure levels;

4. Back-bends are useful for the central nervous system and, according to therapists, they aid in controlling negative emotions.

So, if you are feeling stressed out and can manage to find some free time in your daily schedule, go to a qualified yoga instructor and combat your stress in a healthy way.

Sleep

You must be thinking – why are you talking about sleep when stress has deprived me of it? Well, it is true, but consider this – if tonight you do not have a complete night of sleep, you are going to wake up on a wrong note the next morning, all irritated with a headache too perhaps. Is that going to help at all? No way. See, a sound sleep is important. Or else, you are sure to get caught in a vicious circle.

Here is what you can do:

1. Sleep early
2. Keep a pen and notepad beside your head.

Whenever a thought disturbs you, or you remember a task in the office, write it down. This way, you do not have to hold the disturbing thought inside your head.

1. Avoid caffeine before sleep, as it is a stimulant.
2. When you sleep early, set an early alarm for the next morning. You can get up, do a round of meditation or yoga, reach the workplace earlier and take care of pending issues.

Controlled Breathing

Regular breathing exercises and taking a few deep and controlled breaths during stressful situations can go a long way in reducing tension and relieving stress. There is a well explained scientific reasoning behind this – the extra boost of clean oxygen to your brain cells revitalizes your mind and reduces hypertension. You must have noticed that when feeling stressed, your breathing becomes shallow and irregular, and your heart starts pounding against your chest. But with breathing practice, you can control your breathing and take deep, slow and complete breathes, inhaling fresh oxygen and exhaling carbon dioxide, to nourish your system. Deep breathing is effective in stimulating the parasympathetic reaction, which reduces blood pressure.

Now here's a little scientific input. See, there are two types of breathing: chest breathing and abdominal breathing. The basic aim during stressful situations is to concentrate on abdominal breathing, or more precisely, breathe by contracting your diaphragm.

You can excuse yourself from your desk for 5 to 10 minutes and go to an open area like a terrace or a lawn, if possible. Sit down and just breathe in and breathe out. The best thing about controlled breathing is that it can be done while sitting in your workplace as well. Just a few minutes of breathing will grant you a lifetime for the day's work.

Meditation

Past, present and future – worrying about all three together will never solve your problems for sure. Instead, it will likely add one more to your list of worries – health tensions. Meditation helps you concentrate on the present moment, and daily practice helps you to appreciate patience. When you close your eyes and focus on your present, you can identify and release the factors that cause stress, while also recognizing some causes that you may have been subconsciously ignoring.

Meditation has some simple variations:

1. **Mantra Chart** – You can silently repeat a simple word like 'Om' or any phrase you'd like to prevent distraction and to focus only on your own self.
2. **Mindful Meditation** – Here, you tend to broaden your boundaries. You can concentrate on the whole process and experience of meditation. You can simply shuffle through your thoughts and emotions; focus on necessary ones and discard the rest.

3. **Qi Gong** – This is a traditional Chinese technique of meditation that combines physical movement, breathing, meditation and relaxation.

Before beginning any form of meditation, it is most essential to concentrate on your breathing. When you close your eyes to meditate, focus on inhaling and exhaling. Try to feel your heartbeat and then the rise and fall of your diaphragm. Only then can you be calm and continue further. After all, meditation aims to combine the mind and the soul, whether you are at the workplace or in the snowy mountains.

Visualize

Visualization is a branch of meditation but has its individual uses as well. Whenever you feel stressed, close your eyes. Concentrate on your breathing; once you have your focus, try and visualize some happy memories of your life, such as playing with children or laughing with your parents, or some precious memory with your life partner. This will control the rising pressure within you and calm your nerves.

Worry Time

You can always do something innovative. Create your own 'worry time' to stress out. Yes you heard that right. Allot a time for yourself – say, 30 minutes – for you to channel all the causes of your stress through your mind. See, worries are inevitable. Running away is not an option. And the truth is, no matter how many techniques you apply, unless you deal with your worries, they will continue to stress you out. So, it is better that you face them.

During you 'worry time,' filter all the negative and stressful thoughts and write them down. List and organize them into groups; for example, create a group for thoughts that need immediate attention, another for imaginary problems (and discard these thoughts right then and there), and so on and so forth. This way, you do not have to carry the burden of all these thoughts with you. Whenever possible, take up a problem and solve it. And when you cannot solve a problem, change your approach. Remember, 'I Am Possible,' not 'Impossible'.

Food for Thought

Food is one of the best ways to relieve stress, and a tastier option too. Researchers and nutritionists have identified some healthy foods that can play a role in lowering high stress levels. Moreover, since most of them are small and transportable, you can carry them easily to your workplace.

Cashew nuts and almonds lower your cortisol level, a hormone that induces stress. They are high in calorie content and packed with magnesium. A small packet can always find a place in your bag. Magnesium is a vital nutrient for mental health. Oats have a high magnesium content and the fibers help develop a good mood. So whenever you have a stressful day ahead, leave home with a good breakfast of oatmeal. Eggs are a must in any nutrition list, as they come packed with vitamin B, which helps stabilize moods.

Not only that, but eggs are rich sources of protein too. You can easily pack a hardboiled egg for your breakfast, snack, or lunch. Whole grains stimulate the production of the serotonin hormone in your body, which relaxes the tissues, improves your mood and soothes stress levels.

Broccoli is highly recommended in most nutrition charts. Loaded with folic acid, it prevents irritability and lowers stress levels. If you want folic acid in a liquid diet, orange juice is a great option to have. Bananas are another easily available, portable and highly effective stress busters. They are rich in potassium and regulate your blood pressure, while also relieving heartburns. Omega-3 fatty acids are effective mood elevators.

So when you return home from a stressful working day, a meal of omega-3 will aid in maintaining mental acuity. Salmon and Flax seeds are rich sources of this fatty acid. Cortisol can also be kept at bay if you switch to black tea. Black tea reduces cortisol levels to a great degree and keeps you refreshed and charged. If you are feeling stressed reading this food list, let's try something sweet to make you smile. Sugar helps the body in creating a hormone called glucocorticoid, which counters stress reactions. So, it's not at all harmful to consume a small helping of cookies, chocolates or ice creams to fight your workplace stress.

However, to truly combat stress, also be aware of the foods that you should avoid.

Energy Drinks

Avoid it at all costs when you are stressed. High levels of caffeine make these drinks the worst choice when experiencing stress. They also interfere with sound sleep, which again serves as an aggravator of stress, causing insomnia.

Spicy Food

Stress often leads to a slower metabolism, causing indigestion and acid reflux. Spicy food will in such cases make the situation worse. It is advisable to have lots of water, cucumber, and lemonades to keep your metabolism cool.

Processed and Junk Foods

Processed foods like potato chips contain high concentrations of sodium, fat, and artificial additives, with zero nutrition value. They directly stimulate an increase in cortisol levels and cause further stress.

Alcohol

In a 2011 study, the University of Chicago found that stress and alcohol 'feed' each other. Alcohol stimulates the release of cortisol, increasing stress levels, and in turn, stress reduces the intoxicating effect of alcohol.

Therefore, the next time you grab a quick drink to calm your stress, remember to make the right choice.

Chapter 9

HARBINGER OF RELIEF-

A FEW WORDS FOR THE MANAGERS

Stress not only haunts employees and workers but is an equal headache for managers and employers as well. Being a manager is not a piece of cake, and as the line goes, "with great power comes great responsibility." They often have to endure adverse situations and are frequent victims of stress as well.

For managers, the one critical thing that keeps them on their toes is the productivity and output of the workers. The demands of the company rest on their shoulders, as they are answerable to both their employees as well as their own bosses. To keep the workplace running smoothly, and also to deal with workplace stress, the following few guidelines can help immensely.

First and foremost, your means to communicate to your employees should be both firm and friendly. The workers should get the feeling that they may approach you with their problems without hesitation, but at the same time, respect you too. Try not to be mean spirited.

Secondly, try to keep the workload suitable for the workers according to their resources and abilities. Rewards and incentives will help create a positive competing environment. Praise a good performance and show that the work is valued.

The promotion of an entrepreneurial working climate will provide employees with good control over their work. When workers are happy, they will give 100% to their tasks. A light working environment will lessen the chances of employees holding a personal grudge against the manager. You can go home in peace and arrive to work relaxed, always knowing that you will see happy faces at work.

As a manager, you can set an example of a good role model for your employees by taking management initiatives consistent with organizational values. Encourage social interactions among employees for a more unified work force. Promoting a zero-tolerance initiative towards harassment and discrimination will elevate your position in the eyes of your workers.

Chapter 10

SOME FRIENDLY IDEAS

"A PERSONAL NOTE"

Let me tell you, that the very first time I deemed workplace stress to be an epidemic, I actually meant it. Stress never discriminates according to position, status or sex. It is a necessary evil, present in all workplaces. I, too, have been a victim, and from my personal experience, I would gladly suggest a few ideas that you can implement to combat your rising stress.

First and foremost, take a 'time out'. Whenever you feel too stressed, take a small break from your work for 5 to 10 minutes.

However, see to it that the break is not too long, as it will hamper your schedule and 'time management' routine. Remember that? During this little break, take a short stroll outside and breathe in the air. When you continuously stare at your work list or laptop screen, subconsciously or not, tensions rise, which in turn causes stress.

Take a look outside, look at nature. Get out of the congested office environment. You can even go to the washroom and wash your face. Apply water on the nape of your neck and back of your ears. Close your eyes and feel the cooling effect of water for a few seconds. It will calm you down.

Another quick tip for relieving stress is to drink water. Not only is it good practice for general health, but it is also effective in cooling your system. Drink water or fresh lemonade when you feel stressed. However, try your best to avoid caffeine, because it is, after all, a stimulant. If you think a cup of coffee is going to calm your nerve, it is only going to be counterproductive.

You know, if a garden blossom's with flowers, it looks attractive and also soothing. Do a simple thing and keep your personal desk neat and clean. Keep the files in order, pens in a pen-stand and other important items neatly stacked in drawers. An organized workplace will surely make you feel good.

It will also be easy to find your things when you need them. Another suggestion is to keep a small memento or a photo of your family on your work-table. Whenever you feel stressed, look at it. You can also keep any other items that make you happy – an award celebrating your performance, a keychain from a vacation, your child's favorite toy. Just keep in mind that it should not occupy too much of your table or else it will obstruct your work.

Music is always a preferred way to de-stress. You can tune into a favorite track of yours or any soothing music to calm yourself in between tasks. Another personal favorite of mine that applies more to ladies than men is to keep a bottle of scent with you. It should not be too strong; a mild one is more preferable here, like lavender. The sweet smell will appeal to your nervous system and act as an anti-stimulant to calm your mind. Scents are best used after you have washed your face with cold water. Try it, you will not be disappointed.

One last suggestion – keep a bar of chocolate in your bag. For chocolate lovers, you can keep as many you can fit. You can also carry some favorite munchies, like nuts or dried fruit. Dark chocolate is effective in reducing stress and acts as a relaxing agent. Also, it has been scientifically proven that dark chocolate is very good for the heart, and it also reduces blood pressure. There cannot be a tastier way to reduce stress.

Give these tips a try. After all, as the saying goes, all journeys begin with smallest of steps.

Chapter 11

YOU ARE THE SOLUTION

There are various ways to tackle stress, as we have seen over the course of this book. However, most importantly, it is YOU who can help yourself; it has to be your initiative. Recognize that it takes effort to address the causes of your stress. The effort requires effective communication, control and a willingness to change the circumstances.

Remember, you cannot escape stress, but you can deal with it in a productive way.

1. Stress is a circumstance; you are the force.
2. Stress is not a decision, but to overcome it is.

Consider the '90:10' rule. Just 10% of our life is actually determined by events and circumstances; the remaining 90% is shaped by how we react to them.

So buckle up mate, for you yourself are the ultimate solution to your stress. Say 'No' to workplace stress with a positive attitude. Keep in mind the words Jason Dufner uttered after winning the 2013 PGA Championship: "I do not like stress because stress stresses me out."

New Bonus Chapters on 2nd Edition

I have added a few bonus chapters as on 16th April, 2014.

I have received many emails from people who have talked about their work life and what was causing them stress. I have replied to many emails in these 3 months. Thus, I have decided to summarize these answers and include them in this book.

In the next few chapters you will read a few practical tips on how to cope up with office stress in various situations.

Top 11 Reasons To Quit Your Job To Be An Entrepreneur

Quitting your job to become an entrepreneur? Sounds scary, right?

If your body literally screams everyday to break free from the 9 to 5 routine and cries out for more; then coming up with a strategy to start your own business might be the right answer. But, giving up the security of a full-time job to start your own business can be a very tough move. The fear of uncertainty is the biggest reason people don't end up quitting their jobs. And in no time in history has it been easier to step out and be an entrepreneur.

However, every year thousands of corporate employees are telling their bosses goodbye to start their own businesses. The myth of corporate safety, of rising up through the ranks is over. These mavericks are altering the face of the world as they make an effort to experience the freedom and control they could never taste in a mundane job. According to the Global Entrepreneurship Monitor (GEM), 400 million people around the world call themselves entrepreneurs.

The book, *"The Laptop Millionaire: How Anyone Can Escape the 9 to 5 and Make Money Online"* by **Mark Anatasi** is full of excellent content. I mainly picked up this book enhance my business and i ended up learning much more than I contemplated. This book is a must read for all DOERS.

Entrepreneurship is an intriguing way of life that involves passionately pursuing your business ambitions, fighting for a piece of the market and generating wealth without hunkering beneath a corporate umbrella. Entrepreneurship is incredibly liberating but many people hesitate to take the leap because they fear failure or are unwilling to give up their current professions.

"Risk mens everything from being honest about your faith, to moving, to quitting a job that's paying a fortune but it's not what's in your heart. Risking things is one of the biggest fears we have"- **John Tesh**

Earning a lot of money by working at a job you hate is not worth the money. Being stuck at a job you hate is an awful place to be. A job offers nominal variety in day-to-day tasks and makes the person un-stimulated, demotivated and bored. You must always remember that you did not work through four to five years of college to sit in a cubicle to be a lifeless pencil pusher. You need to work in a lively and dynamic environment where your creativity can thrive. I always had a passion for writing and I knew that in order to be happy and content I had to pursue something that I was passionate about.

"If you think that you are going to love something, give it a try. You're going to kick yourself in the butt for the rest of your life if you don't"- **Joe Penna**

"Show Me The Freedom" does not have quite the same ring as "Show Me The Money", however it could easily be the tagline for a movie about entrepreneurs.

Working at a typical 9 to 5 job is a gratifying way to earn a living for some. Whereas for many others, an inherent entrepreneurial spirit may create a desire to launch a business enterprise or lead them to self-employment. There are numerous convincing reasons that can result in someone quitting his or her job to become an entrepreneur.

At our core we desire more. It's in our veins. Now is the time to work in a more fulfilling career aligned with your skills, interests, passions and to explore new opportunities.

So, are you ready to be next in line?

You could be, if you go through all my top 11 reasons to quit your job to become an entrepreneur. Deciding whether to stick it out or quit your job can be one of the most stressful decisions you ever make. Well, I have rounded up eleven reasons to help you make this critical life decision a little easier. I'm going to tell you why you have to quit your job. Hopefully these points will be instrumental in changing your mind and will give you the much needed boost to take the leap.

- ## **Break free from 'being employed' and taste the essence of 'being engrossed':**

Most office goers find themselves caught between lack of professional growth avenues, ongoing pressures of finding a more lucrative job offer and defiled office politics. But, there will always be people who swear that their jobs provide up-teem satisfaction and growth opportunities that they have always sought. However, the number of such people is very limited.

A self-business model doesn't employ you, rather it engages your dedication. You develop a deep rooted enthusiasm for your work which is a cure for job related problems such as fatigue, stress and many other professional frustrations.

People who enjoy what they do are much more productive than the ones who lack passion for their work. Anyone contemplating towards taking the leap should ask themselves one question- Have I ever been so engrossed in my job that when I look up, I discover that hours have passed in what seemed like minutes? Such immersion is the ultimate key to productivity.

An entrepreneur plans actions, they don't plan results. He or she is a multi-tasker who loves getting it all done because ultimately they get to control the outcome. Starting everything from scratch requires the entrepreneur to create more than the service or product. They are responsible for all the necessities of a company-accounting, sales, capital and operations. Hence, they are engrossed and occupied 24×7.

The book, *"Living The Internet Lifestyle: Quit Your Job, Become an Entrepreneur, And Live Your Ideal Life"* by **Connie Raegen Green** is an awesome read. Green has been doing this successfully since 2006 and she shares her well kept secrets for being able to work from home or from anywhere in the world.

Respect and recognition:

"There are two things people want more than sex and money.....recognition and praise"- **Mary Kay Ash**

Yes, you most definitely want that. You want to feel validated in a way thus far plundered by the regular 9 to 5 job or the corporate world you live in. If you crave the feeling of recognition and accreditation from your friends, family and colleagues; it might just be the right time to become the entrepreneur you always dreamed of.

"People may take a job for more money, but they often leave it for more recognition"-**Bob Nelson**

There is something queer about an entrepreneur's lifestyle which naturally attracts respect and recognition from the society. I believe a lot of people look at entrepreneurs with a bit of wonder and awe, they are somewhat jealous because they are not part of such an elite group. Even those entrepreneurs who give it a shot but come up short earn the respect of the people around them. Atleast they had the fortitude to try and listen to the growl inside.

"Don't worry when you are not recognised, but strive to be worthy of recognition"-**Abraham Lincoln**

• **Leaving The Rat Race:**

Getting up at the same time everyday, struggling through rush hour traffic while commuting from the office, completing the same chores at the same job in the same place with the same people can becoming a grinding experience for some people. It leaves you with little time to take care of yourself, let alone spend time with the family.

By becoming an entrepreneur you cultivate the luxury of creating a flexible work schedule that allows you to attend to your beloved family and enjoy life's luxuries at the same time. If you choose a business enterprise that allows you to work from the comfort of your home, you can avoid the work commute altogether. You will save a lot of time, energy, effort and your productivity will enhance in no time.

Dan Clements author of the book, *"Work-life Balance, Escape 101"*, says *"Leaving the rat race is not as daunting as it may seems.You'll look back in later years and marvel at how easy it was and how much you gained for so little cost"*.

• Freedom and Control:

Most entrepreneurs finally take the plunge into entrepreneurship on the day they become sick and tired of not controlling their own destinies. If the ship goes down, regardless of the time, hard work and talent you've put in- you're out of the door right away. More often than not it happens with zero notice. And even if the ship isn't going down, you're still not the one in control of your destiny.

"Is freedom anything else than the right to live as we wish? Nothing else"-**Epictetus**

The good old corporate umbrella of yesteryear is non existent today. Times have changed and the sooner you realize it, the better for you. You need to build a foundation for life or very soon you will have no roof.

One of the most ideal benefits of being an entrepreneur lies in the freedom to build your business around the life that you choose. There are no chains to hold you down. Isn't it wonderful to work the days you want and take off the days you don't? When you own your business, it's your gig and you are the boss. You can do whatever you want, wherever you want and with whoever you want. You can work either from the beaches of Costa Rica during summer or the slopes of Vermont during winter.

Instead of letting your work dictate the life you're supposed to live, you have the freedom to pursue the life you dream of without worrying about your monotonous job.

I loved the book *"The Four Hour Work Week"*, by **Timothy Ferris**. It is one of the best books that I have ever come across. It has altered my perception of life and work. It challenged me to evaluate my perspective of good living. Tim politely suggests that all people should consider other means or styles of leading their lives, instead of working strenuously and consistently towards an eventual and inevitable retirement. Live like there is no tomorrow. He has laid down all his ideas on outsourcing all our tasks and making more time and space to enjoy ourselves. The notions and concepts that he dishes out to would-be entrepreneurs are mind-blowing. He simplifies all the complexities and demonstrates how to lead a hassle-free and adventures life. Reading this book was a breathtaking and rejuvenating experience. He is a serial vagabond, who works on the move and only for four hours per week and still makes enough moolah to enjoy all the good things that life offers. After all, who doesn't want to outsource the workload and head off to the Bahamas!

Opportunity:

All entrepreneurs have the awesome opportunity to create something that never existed before. Innovator, risk-taker, multi-tasker or an opportunist- numerous names can be used to describe an entrepreneur. An entrepreneur recognises that a particular situation presents an opportunity to make money and goes for it. Opportunities could be limitless; it could be offering ice cold bottles of water in the middle of summer or selling umbrellas on a rainy day.

"Every single person I know who is successful at what they do is successful because they love doing it"-**Joe Penna**

Entrepreneurs are backed by innovation and easily convert a threat or a challenge into an opportunity. As an entrepreneur you will have the prerogative to materialize any opportunity or idea into a successful business venture whereas as an employee you are not entitled to any such possibilities. As an entrepreneur you can choose the people you work with and as your own boss you also have the ability to create your own opportunities. Entrepreneurship also enables you to create opportunities by doing various productive activities such as networking with like minded people, attending conventions and much more. In doing this you shape your own destiny.

The Book *"Living A Laptop Lifestyle"* by **Greg and Fiona Scott** is down to earth and presents internet marketing as a real business full of challenges but one that is very lucrative if you carefully heed his examples. This book is extremely influential for anyone interested in internet marketing. If you are new to this or thinking about internet marketing as a way to build passive income then get this book and read it.

A 9 to 5 job denies you all the growth opportunities. Your employer or boss always tries to keep you down and pays you only enough for you to survive and he or she will eventually replace you anyway. As an employee you will rotate between insults and compliments and stay like a fish caught on the bait. We all have the same 24 hours each day. Is that how you will spend yours?

"The entrepreneur always searches for change, responds to it and exploits it as an opportunity"-**Peter Drucker**

• You will stop being vulnerable:

One of the many reasons why you never hear entrepreneurs complain about the fast changing industry is because they are often the ones changing it. They keep their eyes on the next step, sometimes the next ten steps and always make sure that they stay pertinent. It's an awesome way to make sure that you are never discarded.

Outsourcing, technology, increased productivity effectiveness have all been instrumental in gradually replacing the working class. Most jobs that existed 25 years ago are not required now. Currently CEO's mostly discuss about coming up with good strategies to fire all the daed weight. It is happening across every sector of the economy, everyone is getting fired rapidly. Most people hope that they will work smoothly until they retire when they get a job. Currently that scenario has completely altered. In the current state of the economy job security can be guaranteed to no one. Most employees are now at the pity of the economy and their employers. They are progressively vulnerable. But, by deciding to be self-employed you are in control of yourself. And with control you will have peace of mind and work security.

According to the Pew Foundation, 39 percent of entrepreneurs reports complete job satisfaction versus 28 percent of those who work for a boss. This greater job satisfaction spills into the rest of their lives and has a lasting effect. Another recent study in the University of Sussex, Uk revealed that transitioning from wage employment to self-employment boosted people's overall life satisfaction for as long as three years after the transition.

Self-employed people are happier because of the freedom that working for one's self permits. So lucrative is the opportunity to be one's own boss that many studies show that you have to pay people twice as much to get them to work for others and still have the same level of job satisfaction as being self-employed.

The book, *"Click Millionaires: Work Less, Live More with an Internet Business You Love"* By **Scott Fox** is very intriguing. This book will give you a very good foundation for starting and expanding an internet based business and enjoying the life of your dreams. It contains some excellent advice about starting a brand new business. Too many people fail because they do not adhere to the lessons taught by Scoot Fox.

Pursuing Your Passion:

You may be a creative person who is stuck in a non creative career. For example, an accountant may be a writer or artist at heart. By becoming an entrepreneur you can easily pursue your passion.

Almost everyone has a passion that they want to pursue. But the main problem is, we often push those passions aside in the name of being 'practical'. It's far too easy to get pulled into the 'practical' career and be unable to extract yourself from it later on. It is too convenient to keep doing whatever you're doing while all your passions go into the 'maybe someday file'.

If you simply put aside the 'fear of the unknown', then quitting your job to follow your passion can have numerous advantages. When you plainly follow your passion, you will most certainly find fulfilment and satisfaction in what you do. You get the satisfaction of doing what you always wanted. Fulfilment is not always about 'money', there are several examples of people who earn massive salaries but don't find any personal fulfilment. This happens because they are not living their passion. In order to be successful you must take prompt action with the sole purpose of fulfilling your passion. By quitting your job you will be capable of pursuing your passion without distractions or hurdles, you will get the opportunity to meet new people from your sphere of interest, explore new places and change your life for good.

"One of the huge mistakes people make is that they try to force an interest on themselves. You don't choose your passions; your passions choose you"-**Jeff Bezos**

• You can leave a legacy:

I don't know the authentic meaning of life, but we do know that we all want our life to have mattered. However, you don't have to start a business to accomplish that, becoming a teacher, raising a family or merely being a good friend are all fine ways of leaving a legacy behind.

But, if you really want to 'put a dent in the universe', then you may want to become an entrepreneur. That's what gave <u>Steve Jobs</u> the podium to change the way we think about technology. It's also what gave <u>Bill Gates</u> the chance to dedicate his life in giving back to the society(through <u>The Bill Gates And Melinda Gates Foundation</u>).

A business is a powerful thing. When you build one, you create the likelihood to provide immense value for people all around the globe. If you build a lasting business it will keep making a difference even after you are gone. By creating something distinct and diverse entrepreneurs want to achieve excellence and create change; to leave a legacy behind.

• **Financial Rewards:**

It is a proven fact that there is no better way to create wealth for yourself then by being an entrepreneur and business owner. However, just because you decide to be an entrepreneur does not mean that you are financially set for life. But if you desire a life with no or nominal worries about money-entrepreneurship is your best ticket.

As an entrepreneur financial security is always within your reach. Let's not talk about hitting a grand slam like Mark Zuckerberg, Bill gates, Steve Jobs, Richard Branson, Mark Cuban etc. I'm speaking about having adequate financial resources to live a very comfortable life.

If you have worked for someone else, you very well know that your employer determines your income level. Even if a good performance earns you a raise, your employer still decides the actual amount. As an entrepreneur there are no income limits. Your income is determined by factors such as, how hard you work, how smartly you market your products or services, how skilful you are at managing your business, and the list goes on.

The money you earn is not the most important thing but rather the ability to be able to make money on your own is praiseworthy. When you realize that you are capable of going out and earning your keep, you get a sense of security and freedom that never comes when working for someone else.

• **Your work is solely yours:**

When you work for others, all of your efforts go to helping a business that doesn't belong to you. As an entrepreneur, all your efforts go directly towards increasing the value of your business that you own outright. Receiving a monthly paycheque is fine, but, it is a very short-term fix compared to developing an asset that can bring you enormous wealth for many years to come.

If you live in a free world then there is no reason to work for someone else, these aren't feudal times. The freedom to pursue happiness and live the life of your dreams is the greatest gift of modern society. Yet many people throw that opportunity away.

When you work a job, someone else is in control of your work, responsibilities, salary, schedule and holidays. If you absolutely love your job, perhaps giving up that amount of freedom is worth it. For most people, it seems insane to accept such terms and conditions.

"Your time is limited, so don't waste it living someone else's life. Don't be trapped by dogma-which is living with the results of other people's thinking. Don't let the noise of other's opinions drown out your own inner voice. And most important, have the courage to follow your heart and intuition. They somehow already know what you truly want to become. Everything else is secondary"-**Steve Jobs**

• There is no dull moment:

All organisations hire people only to fill one single role. As an employee, you are expected to do just one thing, it may be efficient, but, it's extremely monotonous and demotivating at the same time.

Entrepreneurs do not face this problem. Instead of filling one single role, they are required to fill almost all of the roles for their enterprise; it is more common with start ups. In just one day you will end up working as the writer, designer, coder, manager, decision maker, innovator, marketer and even janitor. Playing so many parts at the same time by one single person can be challenging, but it keeps things very interesting.

You can discover your true calling by learning something   new   everyday: Personally, I adore the sense of accomplishment

I get when I learn something new, I love the fact that I constantly challenge my mind and keep it sharp.

One extraordinary benefit to having the varied duties of an entrepreneur: there is always something new to learn everyday. If one day you master everything involved in making money online, you would still have more to learn the next day. As an entrepreneur you have to keep up with new upcoming techniques, trends and technologies and the more abreast you are with all the latest metamorphosis, the easier it will be for you to be successful.

People mostly know what they want to do in their lives by the time they are 5 yrs. old and aren't very sure about it by the time they are 25.

Entrepreneurship is a very diverse and self paved career path, so, if you are looking for some clarity on the subject then you might consider becoming an entrepreneur. It is a great way to discover your true calling. Personally, I adore the sense of accomplishment I get when I learn something new, I love the fact that I constantly challenge my mind and keep it sharp.

So, there you have it, my reasons behind loving what I do, why I do it and what it means to me to be an entrepreneur.

At the end of the day having that drive will be your most significant key to being an entrepreneur. If you are already doing what you love on your own terms, you can easily achieve what millions are striving for: being your own boss.

Your hands are not made to type out memos on a regular basis or hold a phone up while you talk to people you despise or put papers through print or fax machines. 80 yrs. from now your hands will rot in your grave, so, you have to make sensational use of those hands now, give them the liberty to make magic!

I know many people who are stuck in jobs that they hate, they don't have an escape route in sight. Money should never be the motivating force because your life can never be so fulfilling that you would exchange it for your freedom, happiness and wellbeing. Of course you will always have bills to pay but it may be time to re-evaluate your priorities.

Dreams+work=Success

Happiness solely comes from your own actions, if there is anything deterring you from reaching it then you need to make changes. It may involve certain sacrifices, but if it means pursuing something you love, it will be worth it in the end.

Don't be afraid to step out, you can do it. Break free from the bondage and restraints of your job and be the entrepreneur you dream of.

How To Deal With Difficult People At Work?

Your office is supposed to be the place where you can give your best without having to worry about the world. But it becomes a place where you have to worry the most, when you have annoying coworkers. People come from different walks of life to work in the same office, and each one of them carry their own persona, some of which are not very pleasant. What can you do when you have to deal with these people who give you a hard time in office?

There may be the infamous cubicle intruder, who loves to sit and endlessly gossip, or there could be the "know it all" who loves to flaunt his or her knowledge. Whatever you are dealing with, there is a way to tackle them all.

Here's how:

Give subtle implied signals: I had a friend named Amy who had a notorious coworker, who loved to visit her cubicle while she was busy working. Every time she excused herself by telling him she had deadlines to meet, but he just would not take the hint.

One day I suggested her to make sure that all the empty seats in her cubicle were occupied. I also asked her to pick up her phone and pretend to be busy everytime her coworker showed up. It took him a while to comprehend the hint, but eventually the man stopped troubling my friend. Amy didn't have to do anything outrageous, yet her problem was solved.

Do not counter attack: No matter how much you are tempted to react, keep calm. The last thing you want is to be the "bad guy". Instead of taking their behavior personally, channel your emotions to achieve targets. Stay away from getting into a power struggle and fruitless interactions.

Be witty: Do you have an over indulgent bully who likes to pick at everyone for no reason? This person is perhaps the most disturbing of all as he usually has some kind of authority in the office and he uses it negatively. Do not take his remarks personally, although, he would love to get a reaction from you, devoid him of that pleasure. Instead surprise him with a witty remark. If this person happens to be your boss, then he would be very pleased to see your presence of mind in this case, and you could earn some brownie points here.

My buddy Mark was in a similar situation once. His boss loved to pointlessly pick at him, but this friend of mine was a very calm headed person. He never got agitated, no matter how much his boss jabbed. Occasionally, Mark would say something funny to lighten the situation and his boss started admiring his behaviour. Eventually my friend got promoted despite being the target of the bully.

This is how things work out with bullies. If they find out you are not a pushover, they simply move on to an easier prey.

Find a mid-way: Ever come across a coworker who has received endless perks due to his association with powerful people? Yes, these are the ones who love to brag and may have utilized their authority to threaten some at the office. Do not be submissive. The key here is to find a middle road where you can talk about some of the common interests that you share. You target is to get your work done. This is the best person you can hit it off with. Chances are that, this guy has taken six years to complete his college degree and is perhaps suave and friendly. You do not have to share the same passion for cars or gizmos that he does. You simply have to break the ice and form a connection. This way, this person is tolerable as well as a useful connection at your work place.

Draw clear boundaries: My sister April battled the flirtatious advances of a guy at her work place. She had her dream job and things were going really good for her until this guy started hitting on her. Initially she dodged him off, but the more she did so, the more this guy advanced towards her. Matters got really out of hand when he tried to make a move on her. She had to finally seek the help of the supervisor.

Flirtation at work place could reach the level of sexual harassment. Make sure that you make your concern clear to anyone who ignores your boundaries. If necessary, ask the HR team for help and they will sort it out for you.

Try constructive distraction: You don't want to get involved in the gossips, try to keep yourself busy with distractions. Put on your headphones and get lost in your favorite track, or check out cool youtube videos – anything that would keep you busy and away from the useless banter at your office. When you indulge in gossips, it mostly backfires, so the smartest thing would be to keep yourself busy and engrossed.

Each and every problem has to be dealt with a unique kind of reaction. However, never lose your professionalism and ethics at your work place to fix a certain problem. Also, make sure that you are not the one who is the source of anyone's trouble.

Do not have high expectations from your coworkers at your work place. Each person has his own share of things to deal with, and everyone has their own way of handling things. Make sure that you do not become a target of the bullies and the invaders. Keep a safe distance from the negative or rude coworkers. It is best to keep your interactions completely formal with such coworkers. If someone is being overly critical, do not get defensive, and do not participate in that conversation either. When the authority senses any sort of urgency, they will step in and take proper action.

Ten Ways to Overcome Office Politics

Office politics is a working example of two infamous social, biological, evolutionary and anthropological theories, one being the renowned "Survival of the Fittest" theory which was sustained by Sir Charles Darwin, and the other one being the concept of the "The Rat". Both are reflective of many things that prevail at a large extent in the status quo, although the concept of Competition and Establishment of Power can be attributed as the driving force for Politics at your work-place.

Office Politics is often used in a negative context, where it involves a person or group of people indulging in activities that may pose to be advantageous to them at the cost of others. "Follow the herd mentality" and the very societal segregation of the perceived "strong" and "weak" are the main reasons for the continual sustenance of 'Office Politicking'. As long as there is an organizational structure, clashing of minds and a number of workers, the place of employment is susceptible to raging fights.

Office Politics can be channeled and used in your advantage. Once the system and the leader(s) of the herd are challenged in a smart way, you can build your way to the top.

The flip-side to this phenomenon are gossip, rumors, dishonesty and rivalry, all of which make for a brilliant book or movie, but can be disastrous for a work-place. All great business patrons agree that the entire organization's synergy is vital for the achievement of its goals, and individual aspirations, especially clashing individual aspirations are detrimental to the business entity.

The same patrons have taken a step back, and do agree on this: While office politics may adversely affect some aspects in an organizational entity, it breeds healthy competition, and while such hierarchy exists, office politics very much has a seat in the front row.

They may take the form of false rumors, bullying, and even sabotaging assignments, so what can one do to deal with such occasions?

#1. Shut out the gossip, and stay away

A great man once said "If gossip were food, most of us will be overweight"

Sure, gossip seems harmless and fun when your colleagues offer you some juicy bits about Mr.XYZ's life, make sure you try to change the subject in a subtle manner. The whole "evils of gossiping" lectures tend to hurt people's ego and they might just rail against you.

Say for example, the group is talking about the department head, Ross's weird habit of going out during lunch hour every day, but how he comes back to his table to eat lunch after, don't directly comment or involve yourself into the entire speculation segment here. Instead, shift to the the topic of what happened to you during lunch, or some things that Ross might've done etc. And then, comment on it.

#2. Detachment is key

Office politics often takes shape because of group-ism. Groups are formed because of identifiable and homogenous traits, skills, interests or ideologies amongst people across a particular spectrum. When one is able to shy away from the eyes of the eagles and vultures, they can successfully remain under the radar and do their respective jobs. Simply staying away and taking every-thing with a pinch of salt is one bullet-proof way to stay clean of messy politicking.

#3.Don't let matters of "Confidence" stray away

Secrets exist everywhere. As long as there are sacrosanct concepts such as "loyalty", "trust" and "ethics", one can be sure that they will be on the receiving end of these 'confidential matters' during their tenure of employment. Just like rumors, leaking of such matters can cause firestorms in the organization.

Being trustworthy is one trait everyone aspires to possess. Make sure that when you are the recipient of such a secret, you keep it to yourself. There is always a chance that if it gets out, it can be traced back to you, and this will cause unnecessary problems, not just among colleagues and peers, but also amongst the superiors.

If someone confides in you, it is best that it stays with you. After all, secrets are to be taken to the grave.

#4.Professionalism, Professionalism, Professionalism

Professionalism, in its essence means to try to be cordial, punctual and have a more or less friendly relationship with those around you.

This is one of the key ways of dealing with Office Politics effectively and efficiently. One needn't be hostile or over-friendly with his peers, as both the extremes attract immense attention, but being professional assures those around you that you are serious about what you do.

#5. Join the game
If you chose to deal with Office Politics by running away from it, one must understand that it will never work. The more you shy away, the more you will be backed into a corner and shunned.

The one way to use it in your favor is to simply play the game. This does not mean you have to be mean, vicious, alert and scheming all the time. What this essentially means is that you must learn to have sound judgments and foresight to pick up on what is happening in front of you and counter it by networking and building a spotless image of yourself.

This means that you start connecting with the right people who will back you up during trouble.

#6. Deducing the hierarchy:

Here, the word "hierarchy" refers to those who hold the highest positions in your team, in terms of intelligence and influence. What is more important is to see how they use it to influence others. Figuring this out is the key to knowing who is most liked amongst your colleagues.

And the premise of politics is influence, not exactly position; therefore building a rapport with the chief influencers is essential.

#7. Remembering the focal point:

Often in Office politics, groups may fight over ways to complete a project, the means to do it or even how to divide the project amongst themselves. It might also happen that you are stuck between two rival groups who simply can't come into an understanding. What do you do then?
One thing that you should NOT do is taking sides. Focus on the objectives of the project and the organization, even if you prefer one group over the other.

Give both the groups a dispute-resolving meeting, where they can express themselves without being a forum for direct insults or fights. At the end, you gain both the party's trust.

#8.Place your name "HERE"

In a meeting if a supervisor asks you about your work updates, make sure that you include all the details. In a conference always give your valuable opinions and suggestions and carve out a place for yourself in the minds of both your superiors and your colleagues. This will help you to earn a position where people will not only respect you, but you might just find yourself being at the top of your league, without conforming to a group.

#9.Fall-back options:

Supposedly, you have already chosen sides and you find that your work and opportunities are being sabotaged by your rival group, then what? Is it too late?

Not really, trace your steps back and approach a neutral colleague or superior and explain that XYZ is trying to sabotage your work and seek their advice on the matter.

Confrontations lets the perpetrators know that they should mind their own business.

Also, have friendly connections with like-minded individuals who will be ready to back you up in a tough situation, a friend in need, is a friend indeed.

#10. Documentation:

Like with uncontrollable situation, it is important that you prove that such incidents that involve unfair and unethical office politics is taking place at your work-place everyday. To point out these instances, one must be able to get a hold of concrete evidence that proves these occurrences.

Once all the instances are documented, it is easy to steer clear of the mess whilst saving the office from some unneeded cacophony. It is essential that one remembers their set of moral values in the office because they will be the only guiding trail of light for a person. Once you realize the fundamental distinction between right and wrong, ethical and unethical, it is easy to avoid unnecessary drama.

Fight or Flee, is a question that you might ask yourself when involved in dirty Office politics, but, it is always essential to under-

stand that over-coming the problem is always better than escaping it.

How To Deal With A Loud Coworker?

Is dealing with an obnoxious coworker the root cause of all your worries? Having a loud person at work can really affect your performance. Studies have shown that those who have to deal with a rude colleague at their workplace are more likely to face marital dissatisfaction and regular conflicts at home. Hence, it is very significant to find a way to deal with them for maintaining proper work life balance.

You can take your complaints to the boss, but the thing is that sometimes people just do it out of habit, and are not really aware that they are annoying someone. In that case, taking the issue to your boss might not really help. However, you can always try and drop some hints. Ask your other colleagues to do the same, so that you are not the only one who grumbles.

It's always better to take charge of the matter and nip things at the bud. You need to let your loud coworkers know that they are raising a ruckus. Take action as soon as possible, as this will affect both your long term and short term productivity at work. If you are having an important phone conversation with your client, would you want your client to overhear your coworker's ranting? I guess that would be too embarrassing and disturbing.

So, take your coworker aside and let them know that they are being way too loud and disturbing others. No one likes to be annoying. Chances are that they will rectify their errors, if you let them know politely.

Answer in the same tongue: We all love music, but it gets annoying when it's played right beside your cubicle at the top of its volume, right? Here's what you can do – throw subtle hints at your coworkers, let them know that they are causing trouble. Ask other colleagues to follow suit and tell them to do the same. Put on ear plugs, and make sure that they notice it.

My friend Amy once faced the same problem. A new guy joined her office, who liked to "break the ice" by playing the hits of Gaga at the top of its volume. Unfortunately she was seated right next to him and his music could be heard from every corner of the room. She was getting frustrated until one day she convinced all her colleagues to pull a prank on him. They made a hand written poster that read "Warning! This place is too loud for work" and stuck it on his desk. As he arrived, all of them put on ear plugs at the same time. As amusing as it sounds, this new guy learnt his lesson and never played loud music again at his work place.

Sometimes small gestures can help a lot to solve a problem. If you are not in talking terms with your colleague, you can always pull pranks to express your discontent. For instance, if your colleague disturbs you by speaking over the speaker phone all the time, mock him, repeat what he does. But make sure that he gets the message.

Request but do not complain: Lastly, if everything else fails, talk to your colleague and explain him the problem you are facing. Start off by complimenting your coworker. Make them feel good about themselves. This way they will trust you more and consider your requests. After you accomplish that, tell them very politely about their annoying habits.

Try to make sure your words sound more like a request than a complaint. You can tell them what you want them to do, instead of pointing out what they are doing wrong. Complaints usually create a feeling of defensiveness. Try to sound as neutral as possible, when you are explaining your problem. When you approach someone politely, they are unlikely to cause any harm.

Two things can happen after that, either they will understand or they will shrug it off and continue to cause trouble. If things get out of control, you should report it to the supervisor.

Try noise canceling earphones: This is your last resort. If nothing else seems to work, technology will always help you. You can always try noise canceling head phones. These head phones are designed to actively cancel out the useless noise around you. These phones electronically generate a certain kind of frequency that creates a buzz in your ears and drives out all the unwanted and disturbing sounds. The buzz is constant, so, it will not be an additional source of disturbance.

There is a chance that your colleague might fathom your problem and do away with their noisy habits. Some people unknowingly disturb others and will change their habits, if asked to. However, while dealing with loud people you have to understand that some people are naturally loud, and they have never been taught how to control this habit. Rest assured, if you have a really loud coworker who is hampering your productivity, the HR team will definitely step in to control the situation.

How To Deal With An Abusive Boss

A long-time friend of mine, Joanne had worked in a firm for over three years in the Research Department. She was a hard-worker, submitted every assignment by the due date and was a more than obedient employee. After the end of the first year, her health started deteriorating. She felt sick often, had migraines and slowly, her productivity went down-hill. One day after work, she was seen running out of the office, crying. She didn't slept for months, she was always distressed and unnerved and when asked why, she always nodded her head in silent dismissal.

Meanwhile, her colleagues stated that their supervisor, Mr.Frederick always seemed to point her out and take a crack at her work, and is always insulting her in front of them, even when Joanne seems to be doing nothing wrong. What's worse, they say that although everyone is entitled to be nominated for an employee award, she wasn't even listed once.

Is this pattern relatable? An American Survey suggests that almost every employee might have faced atleast one instance which they may deem to be "abusive". An important thing to clarify here is to decipher the exact meaning of abuse, and its stature in the status quo.

After all, the nature of the cure can be understood by its potential damages and characteristics.

Workplace Abuse: Is it Legal? Illegal?

The ambiguity of workplace abuse, in all its multitudes is the contributing factor as to why it has been misunderstood by many and hence, it is often over-looked by employees and employers alike.

Remember the time when your teacher might have screamed at you in front of the entire class for no reason? Or the time when you felt that the same teacher was pointedly picking on you for no reason?

"How is this related to workplace abuse?" you may ask, but psychologists state that bullying and being picked on by teachers are the most rudimentary forms of abuse, and this analogy is fundamental in understanding the working of work-place abuse.

Many a times we might've been heart-broken and deeply affected by the reaction and general un-appreciation of the teacher, but is it illegal for the teacher to pick on you, every time? And while we are on the subject, is it unlawful for bosses to keep putting you down?

Prominent psychologist, Dr.Lynn Johnson says that workplace abuse is distinctly different from gender discrimination, racial discrimination and sexual harassment. While these are all types of workplace abuse, these are the ones that can be taken into court, where the offender can be convicted.

According to the Workplace Bullying Institute, we can understand the exact definition of workplace abuse and what can be deduced is that any ***indication of constant intimidation***, ***threats***, any ***attempts of sabotaging work opportunities*** and ***verbal abuse*** all comes under the blanket of work-place abuse.

Revolting, right? However, none of these actions have been ruled as "illegal" in many countries, and thus is the reason for its rampant rise in today's society.

Signs of workplace bullying:

According to Divergent.com, this kind of abuse isn't specifically set to one gender, and what is more appalling is that the most common typeset of abuse is propagated by women superiors towards women, contributing to 60% of workplace abuse charts. The male on male instances of work-place abuse make up 12% of the pie-chart and 30% are the instances of abuse by a male superior towards female employees.

So, now that we can establish that these acts can be perpetrated by both genders, lets check out some tell-tale signs of workplace abuse?

There are a few words associated with workplace abuse, such as:

ISOLATION: The most significant sign of workplace abuse is when your superior singles you out and you are the only target for his constant disapprovals, insults or anger. When a superior behaves the same with all his employees, it isn't much of an abuse, since it could be a major personality flaw. Isolation creates an unstable vacuum of thoughts in the minds of the victim, and it may be liberating to the perpetrator.

REPETITIVE: When your boss yells at you once, he could be having a bad day. Twice, take it with a pinch of salt. If you find him singling you out all the time, you can be sure that it is a form of work-place abuse. Abuse and bullying are repetitive in nature, since it is an intricate amalgamation of one's personality towards another, simply perpetrated by way of their superior job position. Once the abuse has been identified, it's important to know how to confront it and deal with it. Here are a few ways:

There are NO perks of being a wallflower:

One of the psychological drives of workplace bullying or verbal abuse, is the sensation of dominance. Dominance is often directed towards the more silent, feeble and obedient workers. By exercising any of the acts of workplace bullying, what the perpetrator banks on is the silence of their victim. By standing up for oneself, this vicious link can be dissipated.

When you confront the supervisor, you stand up for your rights and what you are as a person.

And what you are is strong. Establishing this firmly throws a bully off-guard and even builds some respect from their side. When you can sternly state that you are innocent and their actions are causing you distress, the villain might just back off.

Being a door-mat isn't going to solve the problem.

Vantage point for the situation:

Workplace bullying can be difficult to spot, and what is most crucial at this point, is to take a step back and objectively evaluate the situation.

Ask yourself some of these questions:

- Is my boss so harsh only with me or does he behave like this to all my colleagues?
- Is he constantly humiliating me in front of my peers or was it just my work that was not up-to the mark?
- Have I lost out on opportunities and advantages because of his/her so-called "dislike" towards me?

Chances are that if your boss shows apparent displeasure, you might not be the only one to notice it. If this is the case, then it is easier to rectify the situation, since you have like-minded peers who want to solve the issue as much as you. One way to overcome bullying is to stop letting it affect you. That is what the bully wants. Once you are calm, patient and strong-willed, you can be certain that their attitude will not disturb you.

When the going gets tough, call in the troops:

If you find that your supervisor's acts are taking a toll on your health and productivity, it's time for you to take the much needed action.

Work-place abuse may go unnoticed, but they are like weeds in a garden of roses.

When one finds that they are simply unable to stand up for themselves, they can report to the Human Resources Department.

Although these practices may seem "tattle-tale"-like, it is important that you involve people who are designed to solve similar situations before things get out of hand.

After all, most bullies are illogical and irrational, so there may be no use in sitting and trying to sort things out with them. The HR department might be able to get you a transfer or maybe even oust the supervisor.

They say that the one thing every employee wants is a safe environment. Workplace bullying is detrimental to the psyche of an employee, and it is seen that 60% of offices have reported atleast one instance of work-place bullying. Eradicating it is important, as it is harmful to the very foundation of the organization.

After all, looking after your morale is sacro-sanct for your health and development, and if you find that the situation isn't rectified, you can always take your talent and knack elsewhere and be treated with due respect.

Conclusion

Thank you again for downloading this book. I sincerely hope that this book was able to help you to prevent, diminish or withstand your workplace stress successfully. Your excessive stress levels may have been your jailer at the workplace for a very long period of time, but, if you continue following the techniques that are outlined in this book, you will soon become free from its grasp. By adhering to these methods, you will be able to experience a renewed excitement and reinvigorated passion for your work that you may not have felt before. Rejoice in this.

Don't fret if your progress doesn't go as well as you had hoped; most people experience several hurdles and roadblocks when trying to alleviate stress from their lives. Don't stop, but climb further up and overcome every obstacle that you encounter. Very soon, you will see the bright ray of light that shows you have accomplished your objective.

I want to connect with my readers on a personal level. Although, I charge for my consultation, I want to offer a **FREE** consultancy to my first 50 readers. You can ask me any question related to your life. Here's the form: http://bit.ly/askjoemartin

Please review it on Amazon

Finally, if you have enjoyed reading this book and have benefited from it, please take the time to **post a review** and share your thoughts **on Amazon**. I will be very obliged, and it would be hugely appreciated. I want to help people and change their lives, and you can enable me to do that by simply sharing an honest review of this book, so that it can reach many more people.

If you aren't happy about this book or have any feedback, then please send me an email directly at <u>joemartin-book@yahoo.com</u>. I am committed to improving this book and making it as pro-found as possible, so that it can benefit more people and add more value to their lives. I'd greatly appreciate if you send me your feedback directly.

Good Luck!

<u>Image credit via freedigitalphotos.net</u>

By Prakairoj, Grant Cochrane, stockimages, kibsri, jesadaphorn, Ambro, Witthaya Phonsawat, By adamr, By bplanet, Vichaya Kiatying-Angsulee, AKARAKINGDOMS, hyena reality, franky242, imagerymajestic & iaodesign.

61075084R00073

Made in the USA
Middletown, DE
07 January 2018